HOW TO MANAGE

TIME

HOW TO MANAGE TIME

R. KUMAR

An imprint of Manjul Publishing House

Sarvatra
An imprint of Manjul Publishing House
• 2nd Floor, Usha Preet Complex,
42 Malviya Nagar, Bhopal 462 003 – India
• C-16, Sector 3, Noida, Uttar Pradesh 201301 – India
Website: www.manjulindia.com

How To Manage Time

This edition first published in 2023
Second impression 2024

ISBN 978-93-5543-247-6

Printed and bound in India by Repro India Ltd.

CONTENTS

An award ceremony of **"Jewels of India Award"** and **"Certificate of Excellence"** by International Business Council, International Institute of Education & Management, Indian Solidarity Council and Economic Growth Foundation for Outstanding Achievements and Remarkable Role in Financial Services held at Supreme Court, New Delhi on 22nd of February, 2019.

PREFACE

We all know the benefits of management of time in our working, particularly if i talk of people engaged in business may be in goods or of services where the cost of production gets reduced by way of doing more work at the same time against fixed cost and accordingly, benefits get an increase. Intentionally i would not try anywhere to elaborate much about the need for time management in this book except where it correlates to the meaning of the phrase. I am not going to write here that 'first determine your aim/target as these all are immaterial for a business concern.'

Further even i wouldn't write about those methods of time-saving that start from the planning of the work, set priority of same work, determining action plans relating thereto, lay of standard time required for each action, analyses of each action, implementation of improvements therein along with the removal of unnecessary actions and achieving the goals of that enterprise.

To emphasize more, rather i would try more broadly on those bigger policies or plans that would add efficiency in the organization's system and in working going on thereat. Separate policies can be made in small branches like improvements in each and every movement of actions, break or rest time, proper training or making appreciation to efficient workers etc. All these are good no doubt and should continue to be carried out in every business entity.

But we are to create such a system where efficiency of doing the work enhances by default or say by auto mode as loss of time is the loss of money. For this, we are to look into those above level situations, working atmosphere, management's planning & their administration style in a particular organization that bring fastness as well as minimum use of resources in the execution of every work of every level towards achieving its mission. My next writing would explain how & what the areas (that directly or indirectly get affected either in the right direction or in wrong) must be touched by the top management in their work plan. These areas have been identified from the core working as well as in deep understanding the behavioural aspects of human beings with the possibility of scientific psychology might affect the workforce.

ACKNOWLEDGEMENT

First and foremost, praises and thanks to the God, the Almighty, for His showers of blessings throughout my research work to complete the research successfully. During the course of my writing, whenever I got frustrated or felt discouraged due to non-finding of new ideas, it remained his blessings with extended hands towards my countdown courage.

I would also like to acknowledge those circumstances which I have realized during my professional career and found that certain things could be much better, had the matter did not taken in a particular way or one's line of actions remained else than taken at that time. These things lead me to pen down all my experienced situations and do a little effort towards the whole business society and ultimately to our nation also. I believe that sometimes discouraging moments become the path of your motivation to do some extra and unique work for society or for some class of people. The only things that one needs to do at that time is to put your all efforts to convert the adverse situations in opportunities for himself as well as for others.

Finally, I am much thankful to my family for their love, patience and prayers to complete this research work.

—Ca Rajeev K. Garg

1

IMPORTANCE OF TIME SAVING OR MANAGEMENT

Disneyland was built in 366 days, from ground-breaking to first day open to the public. Source: (https://pdfs.semanticscholar.org/24ed/0ef476a6e997698ffcfeeed0b567f8377049.pdf)

Not only private entrepreneurs, but various governments and semi-government departments are also busy implementing processes aimed at better optimization of time in their offices and for their people. It was with this aim that the concept of automation was implemented earlier. It also explains the move to usher in digitalization in all the areas of activities. Needless to say, these steps are necessary if a country desires to keep pace with other countries in the international arena. Several instances of various countries where a high level of digitalization is being implemented can be brought to bear in verification of this. As far as India's march towards digitalization is concerned, the present dispensation has initiated a number of steps such as actively promoting online payments, implementing FASTag system at each toll plaza in a bid to save the time of passengers on highways, faceless e-assessment of all income tax cases to save the time of government staff as well as of assessee and his/her counsel by eliminating the necessity of physical presence, and now introducing online e-invoicing for each sale that would ultimately do away with the need of filling sale returns under the Goods and Services Tax (GST) system for the entrepreneur. We can imagine is being saved due to the process of digitalization. Nonetheless, the government is striving hard to save more time of people as well as of its staff. The future belongs to Li-fi instead of Wi-fi whereby as soon as one enters his home and turns on the light, internet connection gets automatically established for use by him.

As regards comfortable or stress-free hours, it is something that everyone desires. Nonetheless, it is not possible for everyone to attain it. It is for this reason that time must be efficiently managed, just like of a valuable commodity. The purpose of this article/book is to provide you with practical tips to help you save time every day while running your business. By the end, you should feel empowered and achieve a lower cost of production as you better manage your time.

Implementing simple, elegant and innovative measures to ensure that the time of your business is used efficiently is always a lucrative proposition. It is imperative to strike a balance between time and overhead expenses as time saved implies reduction in cost. By controlling these two factors in your organization's favour, you would certainly be able to win the battle against your competitors in the market.

2

FLEXIBILITY- NOT RIGIDITY IN WORKING SYSTEM, ELIMINATING UNNECESSARY ACTIVITIES

In this chapter, I have combined two topics in one chapter. These include the elimination of unnecessary activities involved in any type of working and simultaneously keeping flexibility for a change in respective areas of work. Sometimes, the atmosphere at the workplace happens to be such that no employee is in a position to put forth suggestions to improve either the course of action or the system out of fear that he or she might cease to be part of that system. The fact remains that the same work could have been completed in less time had the tasks been carried out in a different manner. Unlike private organizations, such problems are more common in government offices where the problem remains unresolved until the decision making authority finally realizes that certain changes have become necessary to efficiently run the system.

For instance, there are several government departments where different employees are engaged in the same work resulting in a duplication of effort or in certain activities that are serving no benefit. Yet, the old system is perpetuated by the employees under the belief that any effort to change the existing system might call for unforeseen risks whose responsibilities would be entirely on the shoulders of the one who implements that change. In view of these risks, no one makes suggestions about the need for changes and continues following the same pattern of work.

At the same time, getting rid of unnecessary activities is not a viable solution until another option is made available to the executor. In other words, he or she should have the choice of moving to a faster method and discarding the previous method. It is for this reason that I always suggest first putting forth a practical option so that the executor has the option of choosing the time-efficient method. So, it has become the need of the hour that organizations amend their pre-established system in view of the facts of the situation. For this, it has to set aside its rigid approach and adopt necessary changes in the system as early as possible.

Summary

Everyone will agree that systems are good. However, the best system for carrying out work is always preferable and is certainly in the interest of the organization concerned. Nonetheless, it is also agreed that there is always a scope for improvement. So, nothing should be deemed to be fixed forever. All systems are created by human beings - whether or not such systems make use of electric or mechanical equipment. As such, the possibility of mistakes cannot be eliminated, as no human being is absolutely perfect.

3

CLEAR CUT DUTIES & RESPONSIBILITIES

One should be absolutely clear about the responsibility he is expected to discharge apart from certain exceptions that may arise occasionally when he or she has to perform certain tasks outside the domain of his/her specified areas of responsibility. Leaving such exceptions aside, this chapter focuses on what duties one needs to perform and when. The tasks that an employee must perform each day should be as clear as possible. Once the duties are precisely defined, the next step is determining time management practices – whether they are efficient or not. To put it simply, one cannot expect efficiency in work from those engaged in the task unless exact duties are specified. Usually, the concept of clear duties and responsibilities is witnessed in the corporate sector where the policy of the management becomes the basic reason for good productivity. This is further helped by the expertise of people engaged in that field of activity who execute the assigned task as per job allocation chart.

Frequent changes in job-related responsibilities of staff – irrespective of whether they are workers, executives or managers – should be avoided at all costs, particularly when the period is very short. How does it work? Let us take ourselves as an example. Won't we like to perform the predetermined task that is already in our minds, or for which we are mentally prepared, having done that work routinely over a certain period of time? In order to perform that task comfortably and in a time-efficient manner, we go into minute details of that task, comprehend it properly and eliminate all the difficulties that are routinely encountered. Eventually, it becomes less stressful for us. Going through a certain routine gradually brings several improvements in our action plan, as we become used to specific activities involved in the completion of the routine work. Once, we are clear-headed vis-à-vis our assigned task, and we have also found a way around the complexities involved thus making it less stressful, isn't it more than obvious that the same task would be accomplished in less time than before? There is scant doubt in this regard because we have not only thoroughly understood the precise nature of work, but also developed certain techniques under the present system to perform it accordingly.

To understand this concept in an easier way, let us take the simple case of our household. If one already has a fixed schedule of what is to be prepared for breakfast, lunch and dinner the next day, it would consume very less time. In contrast, it would lead to immense chaos if the mother asks from the members of the family about what to cook for breakfast, lunch and dinner on the night before or in the morning. She has to then look for recipes accordingly. Besides, all the ingredients need to be arranged. In the absence of a proper schedule, the level of chaos during all the three meals of the day can only be imagined when every family member places a demand for dishes of his/her own choice. The matter would not end there as the subsequent discussion might involve arranging the ingredients. Further, if the ingredients are not readily available, the members would deliberate on who should be sent out to fetch them - if it is raining then whether the elder son or the father would drive the four-wheeler to the market. Now, the amount of time and energy consumed by the family of four or five in the absence of a clear schedule just in the preparation of three meals in a day can only be imagined. Had there been a pre-decided menu in the family, it was likely that mother alone could have cooked and served all the three meals ready to eat sans any discussion that otherwise occupied the family that day. This would have been possible because she would have arranged all the required ingredients on the Sunday of last weekend.

The same situation happens in business when the

duties of an employee are not clearly defined (just like that of the mother in the absence of a schedule in our example). In such cases, he and other employees - both senior and junior - waste their time in unnecessary discussions and solving new problems that would spring up when work is being finalized at the current moment. Not only the concentration required for discharging a task is lost but other resources of the organization are also wasted while productivity goes for a toss accordingly due to non-clarity with regards to the work to be done by the staff.

However, a change in duty is considered beneficial and in the interest of the organization when the objective is to acquaint team members with the working of a particular department, particularly when skilled/semi- skilled people go on leave. In such situations, work in the organization does not suffer, as there are other staff who can always act as standby for discharging that work in the absence of on-leave employees, who were performing the task earlier. Such a standby arrangement helps the organization in handling tough situations not only when the employees concerned are on leave but also when there is frequent staff turnover in that business entity.

Summary

When the word CLARITY comes, the word CONFUSION gets over by default.

Savings in time can be much enhanced when one knows exactly about his duties and responsibilities in a clear manner. Keeping the target of completion of the work in his mind, he finds out the easy and fast way of doing that job. In ancient times, when people were not so educated in new and fast techniques and kind of work were very few, even then they found out very beneficial techniques of doing that job may be in agri-sector, Mechanical sectors or in other manufacturing activities. A number of working techniques that had been used and developed by them even have their place in today's modern scenario with new forms or shapes. The purpose behind mentioning all the above is that when one knows about his work, he concentrates wholly upon that and finds out the right line of actions, which makes the job easy, accurate and last but not least, less time consuming so that extra work can be done at the same time.

4

CLEAR CUT RIGHTS & AUTHORIZATIONS

Yes, many people perhaps would not easily accept the concept of clear authorizations that may directly benefit in saving time for the management. Nonetheless, it surely helps in saving time indirectly in the completion of specific tasks.

What happens when there is confusion pertaining to our rights and authorizations? In such a situation, we are not in a position to take immediate or quick decisions owing to an absence of clarity with regards to our rights. It can also be one of the reasons for loss to the organization, as the person involved in the task since beginning could have taken a call and accomplished better results for the simple reason that he had been familiar with it from the outset. On the other hand, other people might not be well-versed with the entire situation. Consequently, the entire team is unable to proceed further even though a major portion of the captioned work had already been completed by it, and is forced to remain idle until the instructions come from the higher-ups. Here, I am not implying that the whole team does not or can't do any other work during the period until the decision comes from the superior who has the authority to decide on the matter. However, it is certain that the time of the idle workforce would be utilized either in some other routine or non-routine work instead of putting in efforts in the high-priority task at hand.

It is important to understand that this results in the team being unable to prove its work efficiency in both the first assignment where the decision was delayed, as well as, in the new assignment, in which they put half-hearted efforts, until they are supposed to work continuously. As has been explained above, one can comprehend the the level of time efficiency that would be attained as a result of non-clear authorizations either in earlier work assignment or in the new one.

Lack of clarity in power and authorization leads to another type of loss as far as efficient time management is concerned. It involves such situations wherein decisions to be made entail certain risks but the manager concerned dilly-dallies it on the excuse that he is exactly authorized to make the decision. He puts the onus on other managers who he thinks can take a call on the issue. So, either other members of his team or his seniors should come forward to make the decision, as they have been empowered by the top management. To avoid such situations, it is highly recommended that responsibilities be assigned to the employees concerned along with a vesting of power - much like it happens in our armed forces where soldiers execute the commands to precision in strict respect of rules, not leaving the smallest detail unattended.

Summary

This is something that you will often encounter in your work - even if you are running a small business or a shop with just four or five employees belonging to the unorganized sector. In case any work has not been completed by any of them in your absence, he makes a simple excuse: "I had not been asked to do that job. Someone else did it the last time. So, how could I have done it now when there were no clear instructions to me." The fact though is that the very employee was competent enough to execute the task had he applied his mind and arrived at a decision. Fixing clear duties, as well as rights, require a high-level of concentration based upon past experience, nature of work handled and practical situations that might arise from time to time in one's business in addition to other factors. However, exceptional cases can't be ruled out altogether wherein experienced staff may be required to arrive at a quick decision depending on the situation to avoid waste of his time as well as that of his team.

5

CLEAR WORK – WHICH IS TO BE DONE

Out of the number of tasks required to be carried out – maybe at same premises or at different work stations – both the working team as well as the head of the department should be clear about the tasks that need to be carried out simultaneously. This helps the entire team plan accordingly. In its absence, neither any work would be completed up to the desired level nor would the top management be in a position to measure the efficiency of the working team.

If measurement of efficiency becomes hard to calculate, then how one can implement time management techniques for the work in question and reach the optimal level of cost. In this view, it becomes necessary to decide on the work or works that are to be started first. A product under the work-in-process stage may require a number of operations within the same premises, which can be started depending upon either the convenience or the discretion of respective supervisors. But a production schedule is still required so that the output of each segment can be compared with standard parameters laid down before the start of production. And neither the operational team nor the management can create confusion by saying that we have started multiple works at the same time and are unable to calculate work performance as all the process is in the semi-finished stage.

If we take an example of a real estate developer, who is constructing a number of towers consisting of hundreds of commercial offices as well as residential houses. Now, which tower should be taken up first. Or, should it launch construction of two or three towers simultaneously in the first phase of construction. Likewise, he needs to decide on which towers would be constructed in the second and third phases. All this needs to be planned out at the very first stage of starting the construction keeping in view the agreements with the buyers, date of final possession of flats and registration thereof in favour of those buyers. If all this plan had been settled earlier, then work can be started by the team without wasting time in any type of confusion relating to work. Accordingly, necessary arrangements of storage space, water and electricity supply, construction of roads towards that particular tower - whether it should be built by using mettle or mud, and whether it should be made temporary or permanent, considering the next plan of construction in mind, we get ready to start the work. The working team then makes their plan as per the above construction schedule and also prepare sub-plans to meet out the whole work at different stages. Such pre-planning of work wouldn't only save time of the working team but also reduce various other costs that have to be incurred whenever construction of a new tower starts - as indicated maybe on temporary roads, storage space for material, and on the other arrangements, etc.

The above is an example of a big project where a lack of a clear work plan or schedule perhaps does not generally happen. I have quoted the above case just to understand the captioned chapter completely as well as to correlate with our own case to the extent applicable. When such type of exercise would be implemented in every organization, then definitely much time could be saved in completion of each work and also clear scheduling of work can also save various other costs that occur due to non-scheduling of work.

Summary

Clear work refers to an exhaustive term which denotes the overall work plan of a business entity while clarity about duties refers to the work that each member of the team is supposed to have in his/her mind to perform as per the instructions of the management. So that every member of that team performs his duties perfectly and efficiently without creating any type of chaos while doing their jobs with other members of the team. Many times, it has been observed that a team has been instructed to do one work and all arrangements have been made accordingly. But when some percentage of work has been completed or say the relevant work is under process, the same team was again instructed to stop this work and start another one as the plan of top management has been changed. Sometimes, again the same instructions come to stop second work also and start some other work. Such instances waste the good time of working of the entire organization and not only of the respective executing team who was directly responsible to do that work.

6

DO NOT LEAVE THE WORK INCOMPLETE AND START AGAIN & AGAIN FROM THE SAME LEVEL

Time can be reclaimed when we complete the work that has been started first – except in such situations when leaving the previous work and taking up another task would prove beneficial for some reasons. Barring such rare circumstances that may arise during the course of running an organization, the concept of efficient time management requires that the team rounds off the task begun earlier in all respects satisfactorily. In contrast, the performance is bound to suffer when you jump between tasks.

Time can be managed efficiently even under such practical circumstances (as mentioned above) when the necessities at work forces the team to shift from one incomplete task to another whether at the same premises or at a different location. With the application of good concentration, the previous task can be left in such a manner that when it is resumed, it would be with less difficulties and minimum waste of time for the entire team. I am of the view that in the majority of the cases, any production/completion process - whether it be related to manufacturing of a product or rendering a particular service - there remain many small and big segments that are required to be done to bring the product to its final stage. In other words, various sub-tasks have to be completed before giving a final shape to the entire service. So, in my opinion, whenever such a situation arises, we should leave the earlier work by completing certain segments in such a way so that when we start the project again, we may start from the new segment without working on the number of in-completed segments of that project or work. This is so because when we start working on an incomplete segment again, there is a possibility of not being able to recollect or recall the whole work done on that segment earlier. Thus, the time spent on this process would entirely be extra time that perhaps would not have been required had this particular segment been completed. So, this way much time can be saved instead of wasting it while we restart that particular segment if not from the roots but definitely from the next stage.

Now, I would refer again to the earlier mentioned case of real estate development. It could be that the situation demands that the work on a particular tower be left halfway and work be started on another tower. If the civil work on the structure of that tower is completed before leaving the work, then there would be no need to recreate the infrastructure like heavy cranes, temporary padding up to the last floor of the tower and other similar facilities that might be required to complete in structure work of last two or four floors of that tower.

Similarly in service industries, if I talk about an accounting firm, which is forced to leave the balance sheet in between again and again due to the non-availability of certain information from its client, it might be much better if they complete that balance sheet in all respects subject to only those points superseding thereon, for which information is pending till the moment. As such, the accounting firm will need to do only those changes in the balance sheet as and when these reach to them instead of going through the whole balance sheet again and again on getting the pending information either partially or completely.

Summary

Practical difficulties in completion of a particular work, can't be avoided every time. This remains part and parcel of any project everywhere. However, the minimum occurrence of such difficulties remains always beneficial to the organization. But the stage at which this work is to be left should be considered carefully so that the cost of time as well as of other expenses that have to be incurred in restarting the remaining work, may result in a minimum possible level.

To continue an ongoing project, you must review what you have already accomplished, get out all your tools, and decide what you will do next. If a project is almost complete, why not finish it immediately? Sure, you might stay half-hour over time, but you will complete it in less time than if you put everything away to start again tomorrow. Set aside time at the end of the day to wrap up short assignments. The more things you conclude, the less time you'll spend worrying about them.

7

DO NOT LEAVE THE MEETING UNDECIDED AND DISCUSS THE SAME ISSUE AGAIN & AGAIN

As mentioned above, the emphasis is on optimizing the time of not only executive teams but also of senior management to some extent. Now, the higher management is responsible for planning, policies formulations, successful implementation thereof, analysing the results therefrom and long-term thinking of the organization. Saving the time of senior management requires managing the precious commodity in a manner that it could deliver the maximum output in the time available. This not only saves the cost for the business enterprise either directly or indirectly but also makes a good impression regarding the working style of junior staff or other associated people of the organization. This also helps in setting up well-established guidelines for executing the work for the entire team in that organization.

Now, the question arises as to how such a working style can be improved by the senior managers who are involved in planning, policy framing and who have to conduct numerous meetings at different levels. They work in the core area of the organization and others follow their guidelines. In order to make more time available to them to work in the above said areas, they need the best time management in their working style. The strength of such senior managers in numbers generally is low as compared to the rest of the workforce who are deployed at different levels in the organization. But their one decision can either spoil or improve the working of the whole of the workforce there.

To make more time available to senior managers to execute top-level functions, they should make each meeting more meaningful and productive instead of concluding it without arriving at a final decision, instead of putting it off for due one reason or the other. Sometimes, decisions could not be made due to the non-availability of sufficient information, explanations, or other documents required for any decision in that meeting over the captioned subject. Similarly, sometimes common consensus couldn't be arrived at as everyone had different views. Non-attendance of the meeting by all the concerned sometimes becomes the reason for non-decision and meetings have to be fixed on the next convenient dates which were not so easy perhaps. If I do not go much in detail of why the decision could not be held in any meeting rather stress more on actually what has been done in that half or quarter complete meeting, would it not be right TO LOCK AT LEAST THOSE POINTS WHICH HAD BEEN DISCUSSED THERE, COMMENTED BY ALL THE PRESENTEE AND A COMMON DECISION HAD BEEN DRAWN OUT THEREFROM? By this exercise, there would not be any need to re-open that particular topic in the next meeting and the same time can be spent on some other important issues. Although such practice might already be in use in high professional concerns in mid-level or say a closely-held number of companies, time is being wasted on again and again discussing the same issue in frequent meetings might be started from some other corner. The effect of the same happens that every time some different results or decisions come out ignoring our own decision that had been taken earlier.

In some of the cases, I have seen that meetings of top management are being regularly scheduled with a small gap of days or weeks may be on fund management, financial profitability, status of the organization, or to see the viability of each new order that the organization procures from the market even though the facts that rates and other terms are equally same as that of earlier orders, supply schedule or on the progress of either existing or on the new unit of the organization, etc. This concept remains restricted not only to the meetings but instructions to concerned staff are being passed on to re-make either the fund position, financial status, or profitability aspects or others entirely with new exercise on them. In such situations, it happens that the concerned staff either do a copy paste of an earlier exercise with a new date and name and show how much time has been taken in doing that work or do the entire work again by passive mind and waste so much time in that exercise. Not only restricted to this, but even entrepreneurs or the whole management also do not be able to take one wiser decision in so many meetings on the same issue. This leads to maximum wastage of time of all the HODs, managers, senior teams or of others. My concern is on holding the meetings in such a manner that these avoid wastage of time as well as of overlapping of those discussions which are being held again and again.

Meetings are responsible for a lot of wasted hours. First, if we address the meeting setters, is a conference necessary? Would an email not serve the same purpose? Does the entire team need to attend (because they play significant roles) or only certain members? If you are an employee, it might be difficult to avoid meetings, but your boss might understand if you point out a potential conflict of your priorities in other work of the organization. You might say something like, "The meeting today about the dress code falls during the time I scheduled for Project

Urgent. Since we are on a tight deadline, would you prefer me to work through the meeting and review the notes later?"

Summary

Meetings with the involvement of managing teams on any issue are always recommendable as these not only result in the best decision but also to boost the morale and interest of the entire team. If these meetings remain precise, consistent, short and to the subject matter of discussion, then definitely it proves to be beneficial in the interest of the organization as a number of brains are involved in a particular decision and all have their own knowledge and experience about the market, competitors or of other things. But sometimes as I have seen that entrepreneur himself schedules so many meetings in a day or over the week that the whole senior staff remains busy in getting preparation for those meetings starting from the intimations to all, preparation of data from all departments, engagement of PA or minutes writer, hospitality, etc. Such over-busyness of staff in conducting meetings, leave behind their many works incomplete that were supposed to be completed on specified dates. Sometimes I feel that such type of instructions for unnecessary meetings from the owner's side might be to put pressure on staff or to show one's own impression on them.

Meetings can be essential, but they can also turn into time wasters if they go on too long or happen too frequently. Accept and schedule only important meetings.

Promote virtual meetings to avoid traveling, conference room, hospitality, and unnecessary talks. Otherwise, meetings would be responsible for a lot of wasted hours.

8

PROCRASTINATE-SHOULD NOT BE

I might have mentioned this point either earlier or in the latter part of this book; procrastination in any work of the business, should not be there as it eats away most of the time. This type of working approach habitual by the staff or others may upset the whole smooth running of the business if the same did not exist earlier in that organization. If the same organization is in an expansion plan or in the process of establishing an additional unit with targeted time completion, one can imagine that how much delay be there in completion of that project if the staff is habitual of procrastination. It is a common human experience involving delay in everyday chores or even putting off salient tasks such as attending an appointment, submitting a job report or academic assignment, or broaching a stressful issue with someone. For centuries, human beings have procrastinated in their nature.

It is not that putting off work adversely affects those projects which are bigger in volume and value. In my view, even small work may be of time and importance or of routine nature, affect equally worse as that of bigger. It would not be wrong to say that sometimes avoiding small value work causes greater loss than big projects. Such incidents occur when one is dragging the low-value work continuously but a time comes when dragging it further is not possible and, in the meantime, some important work is also required to be completed which otherwise causes great loss to the business. Now to avoid the local laws, police action, or other forceful actions, small value work has to be completed first and then the loss of a bigger amount due to non-completion of that task has to bear. Putting off those works, which can be easily completed in routine while carrying other works, sometimes reach their peak level and accumulates in good numbers. Now, this pending work starts to create a great disturbance in the completion of other works.

So many cases can be mentioned in this topic particularly when we have to get work done from some government office. Where work gets stuck sometimes due to non-compilation of small work. Such cases involve when documents require approval from government departments before a certain date, completion of all formalities either internal or external for sanction of financial assistance from any state financial corporations or others, and so on. In one case, a subsidy from the state government was available to new units with certain terms and conditions of the Industrial Policy. An organization was well entitled to this and the entrepreneur has issued necessary instructions in advance to the concerned staff for collecting of information either from internal sources or from outside so that application can be filed for subsidy within time. Somehow information from the internal source gets collected but some information was to be collected and authenticated from electricity departments, municipal corporations, and from the Registrar's office also. When time remained very short and information from two or three departments is pending, the whole possible manpower has been involved in getting the same pending works done from above said respective departments before applying for state subsidy. Despite best efforts, all information/ documents/authentications could not be availed from those departments in time due to the number of consecutive holidays in those days. The result was an organization deprived of availing that huge benefit which was a clear profit to that concern along with taxation benefits.

Doing things at last moment always remain expensive that costs to company.

Summary

Avoidance of doing a task that needs to be accomplished by a certain deadline despite knowing the facts that might have negative consequences to the organization is not good for any business concern. Although such types of habits may also be avoided in personal matters. But, in business, top management should be strict enough in handling such procrastination due to all the above-said reasons. Imagine if a teacher promises to take the class for a period every day at a live webcast & also instructs that all should be ready by 9 am with required systems at their home. But every day when students are ready after bathing and dining, he makes an excuse of slippage in mind and adjourns the class for another day. This he informs only when either of the students of the class reminds him about the class schedule after waiting. Sometimes time happens to be 10 or 11 am when he intimates such adjournment. This happens 3-4 days a week. One can guess the level of harassment that might have been suffered almost daily by all the students of that class until the message comes from the teacher. I do not think that those students might be able to put their concentration into studying for the next 2/3 hours at least. Further, if this teacher starts the class after 9 am, say sometime at 9.30 or 10.00 o'clock, what concentration of students would remain in the remaining time of that class. If these situations take place in business, how much time would have been wasted of the junior staff if I ignored harassment for a moment?

9

SET GOOD PROCEDURES & LINE OF ACTIONS FOR DOING WORK

Time can be best managed and saved if steps of doing that work are very precise and towards the achievement of the target efficiently. Work may be of any kind, either physical or mental, which is generally carried by the staff sitting in the office space of the organization. However, there are other types of work that are performed out of the office premises, say work of marketing team, of purchase team to some extent, banking or finance, and, last but not least, liaison work with various government, semi government or other departments. Everywhere time management can be implemented without any assumption that time can be saved only in the **physical movement** of the workforce so that production can be increased with the same workforce at the same time. So, remove all those items that no longer serve a purpose to your mission whether physically or electronically or both.

Generally, a procedure is a set of detailed instructions that tell the reader how to complete a task. Others consider policies and procedures to be interchangeable terms i.e. a list of tasks to complete the goal.

From my own experience, I have seen that maximum stress is usually given on the structural line of any work, whether it be of civil nature, production of goods, electric installation or commissioning of plant and machinery, etc. and efforts there remains to eliminate all the unnecessary actions being performed by the said workforce of the organization. Implementation of professional procedures of doing a respective work increases the production capacity with the same available infrastructure. Usage of Laptop over the Desk computer can save time and work also becomes possible anywhere. Further flexibility of use of the internet remains with the machine used forever. A number of countries are too advanced in setting up either human activities or machines and playing the entire business game over the lower labour cost that comes in producing a product as compared to other countries. Every business enterprise may adopt such good procedures and other lines of actions in their structural work to compete not only in the domestic market but on international platforms also.

The cost which is being incurred on expenses other than directly related to production also impacts the profitability of an organization. If I may digress a little from the subject, good time management in the above said areas other than the production line helps in the completion of work time and all the hindrances get removed in the smooth running of the business. Therefore, determining a proper action plan in the above-said areas is equally important and cost-effective as that of the production area. Good working procedures reduce the need for more staff and people in the business entities perform their duty in a defined manner.

I have seen that there happen to be very tedious procedures somewhere in routine purchase or sales activities. In an organization, requests for preparation of requisition slip first get approved from MD, and then any requisition can be made by the respective department. Interestingly such requisition again goes to MD for his approval and then the Purchase order be prepared by the team. Further, a list of all the prepared POs. of a day is also prepared for the MD office and all these POs. were sent to GM Operation for his signature. What I observed from the above working that the number of times GM himself does not approve those PO in the system rather his assistant does this exercise in the belief that MD had approved twice this requirement by way of Request for preparation of Requisition and Requisition slip itself. Now, will the GM supersede his boss i.e. MD of the company, and reject or add any PO therein? Absolutely No. To the maximum what he can do is, to reduce some quantity in a PO & reorder the same after some days to maintain stock at a minimum level. This would happen very rarely by him just to show his work. Therefore, if he himself does not study all those POs, then where he can be held responsible in case of some errors, if finds out after MD's approvals.

Some flexibility must be there in all the procedures laid by the organization because in routine one may find chances to do the work in lesser time if he breaks those procedures with the permission of seniors. In such a way much time can be saved by ignoring all the line of actions which had been established to do that work. But one thing that should be taken care of is that such overruling should be occasionally at the workplace otherwise infrequent occurrence, it would be better to change that respective line of actions in the system.

Summary

To save time while carrying on any activity, a proper work plan along with a line of action should be established both in production as well as in the non-production area which covers all the activities running in that organization may be of administrative, account/finance, purchase, sale, etc. The traditional approach needs to be changed when only stress was given on the working movements of a particular work. Today, there is a need to lay procedures so that time can also be saved in the thinking process about the work of senior managers.

10

DEVOTE TIME ON RELEVANT WORK MORE AS COMPARE TO IRRELEVANT

Unnecessary or say irrelevant activities from the system, if removed, can save the time of the working staff or labour of that enterprise. Sometimes such savings go up to 40% of the total time taken before such removal in the system. These types of systems are generally found in a mid-level organization where maximum decisions are taken by the entrepreneur himself and no manager happens to be in a position to stop him from doing work which is not required for the business. An entrepreneur might have taken such a decision either in hurry or due to over busyness in his working that he forgets his earlier decision in a similar matter.

In one of my experience with a client, I have seen that whenever any person of a department comes to him with finding some mistakes in a particular segment say in payment procedures, my client immediately instructs him to also check all the payments from today onwards before come to him for the signature ofbank transfer or on cheques. No person out of three/four already involved in such checking is being removed from future checking in the reference when one more staff has been assigned this duty also. If I describe the whole system of payments' existing earlier before adding one more signatory, it was as that on due date a clerk of account department starts to prepare the list of payments to be made on that day simultaneously other clerk extracts the particular bills with all necessary documents from the purchase order and check these bills with the list. After checking by both these persons (one was senior to the other) , they start to prepare set of purchase bills in serial order and also prepare cheques of respective suppliers and send this payment sheet along with cheques and all purchase documents to purchase department for their review and also to DGM Accounts for their approval. Before going to DGM, one senior manager also authenticates that list with payment cheques. Now DGM also takes his time in checking all this and after checking this payment sheet along with other documents sent to GM (F&A) for his authorization also who was added recently in this payment channel when he points out some mistakes in payments. After approval of the GM, all documents come to the MD office where his PA minutely tallies word to word of payment sheet with all those documents and then put to his MD for his approval on sheet. After seeing all the signatures of persons involved in a payment channel, MD approves the sheet for the signature of cheques from different authorised signatories who were authorised to sign the cheques within their set limits (up to 1 lac, then 1-5 lac, then 5-20 lac and then 20-50 lac) which were up to say 50 lacs of four senior managers of the different department other than accounts & finance. Cheques of above 50 lacs were signed by MD himself which were very rare. Before signing the payment sheet, MD also makes sure that only those payments have been mentioned in the sheet which was discussed by the Manager Purchase and Manager Accounts with him.

When all this exercise has been complete till MD signature, now the account clerk rushes to those four senior managers of different departments who were authorised to sign as per set slab of amounts (under intimation to Bank also) for their respective signatures. Somehow, he manages to find each of them at their locations and get their signatures either on the same day or on the other. Now, cheques become ready for their delivery to suppliers. Rarely, when any mistake comes in the knowledge of the MD office, each one takes the shelter under the excuse that the other person must have checked this mistake so I did not check again due to my busyness in other work. However, in future, I will take care of this. When those managers who were authorised to sign cheques were asked what they check before signing the relevant cheques of the payments, all easily say that we are not so concerned to whom and what payment is being done as we are not aware of it. What we do is just to see the sign of MD on the payment sheet and correspondingly sign the respective cheques in favour of parties.

One more experience that I had while working with clients, a number of reports from various departments may be of production with all its processes/segments, electrical, store, costing, along with accounts/finance department etc. be prepared and sent to top management or MD office directly. But for a moment no one considers those reports with care except when exceptional reports are being informed to them. This does not over here, the information contained in all these reports remain almost the same and extracted from one or two common basic sources of information. Senior-level managers involved in these reporting procedures generally waste good time. Had the need for reporting be precise and relevant, much time may be saved if irrelevant reports are informed from the system.

Summary

Pros & Cons of every working step in a system must be considered carefully and may be removed or added if that action is not going to benefit the organization f some kind. Such actions would reduce the time requirements as well as working of the staff also. Consolidation of work under a single task also prove to be the key factor in identifying those who do little but take full time for a job. Replacement of such employees reduces the requirement of more to lesser. Such actions result in lower overhead expenses and increased profits.

11

STRESS FREE WORKING - EITHER OF WORKPLACE OR OF HOME

If we implement the same concept upon us, the final result would immediately get stuck in our mind. A number of times we either had to listen to such learning from our near and dear ones or we ourselves advised others upon the same teachings. Stress does not allow us to do the work with all possible fine results that others may drive out who do the same work with any kind of stress-free mind.

At the workplace, it becomes the responsibility of senior management or of the entrepreneur himself to do away with all those things of the system that are responsible for the creation of stress on the minds of staff or other workers. This may be due to many reasons prevailing there say un-equal behaviour of seniors with their workforce, de-recognition of good efforts, disproportionate in promotion or increments, unhealthy working conditions and so on. To remove such malpractices, the role of the entrepreneur has its vital impact in all these conditions. A rightful direction from him leads the next line of management to establish the system free from above said malpractices and create the working atmosphere in a more satisfactory position where every junior or senior work with great efficiency & acknowledgement. They use their competency from all angles and ever remain ready to try to draw the best results from their working, innovation or motivational spirit. On the contrary, a little direction from owners towards going on above malpractices would gradually increase the bad factors in the organization and number of times, senior staff of next lines of organization's hierarchy be successful in availing personal advantages may be in terms of promotion, appreciation, personal work or to satisfy own ego etc. This all happens due to the green signal from the higher management may be in silent terms if not directly spoken.

Arrangements of some kind are always recommendable at the workplace so that employees may remain stress-free even from home also. However, these are personal matters of the employees and supposed to be tackled by his own efforts. But still if somehow any training like 'Art of Living' or other can be arranged fortnightly or monthly, the benefit would go to the organization when the employee would work efficiently. If an employee is himself of ultimate mind, he should make his/her spouse an equal contributor to the problems which he/she is facing & work under tensions. By this contribution of the family, he/she would be able to attend the workplace without any stress from the family side. Although it is not a part of the job of any management to make such arrangements at the workplace, still a happy & comfortable employee from his/her family puts more concentration in the work of the organization.

Summary

As I have started this chapter with our own implementation of such situations and described possible final results, I think the whole concept is clear itself. At the workplace, such stress takes a toll on one's productivity and health. With a stressful mind, one cannot live his/her life perfectly then what to say about the performance at the workplace.

12

NUMBER OF PEOPLE SHOULD NOT DO SAME WORK- OVERLAPPING OF WORK

If we go by the dictionary meaning, overlapping refers to a situation in which more than one individual is responsible for doing the same job.

When the same work is being assigned to more than one person frequently in the organization, then certainly much time is being wasted in performing that task as a new person would take his own time in starting and doing that job and time consumed by the earlier one would go in vain. Now, if the second person also remains unsuccessful then one another person from the staff or otherwise take the charge of same work performance and restart that job as per his own experience.

Now a question emerges from the above context: Whether our allocation of the job was not proper and in accordance with the capability of either first person or the other. If such is the case, then there is a need to review the process of allocation of jobs. The second reason of such overlapping may be due to the human nature of an entrepreneur or top management who overlap the duties within the organization by assigning the same job to others either when one says that he can do the job more efficiently than his predecessor or some negligence of the same predecessor comes in the notice of job assigner. In both situations, some patience is required, and the policy of 'wait & watch' should be adopted. The earlier who had to devote much of his time, as well as his concentration in completing the work, should be given reasonable opportunity to make the job complete and in case he needs some guidance in the execution of the same that should also be provided because it is not possible that every time work would be assigned to another one. So, training workers becomes necessary to make them be ready for completion of work next time. Moreover, if earlier one has a nature to work, every time he may intentionally behave in a similar manner whenever work is assigned to him under the shelter that last time some other staff have completed that particular job.

Summary

Let the work be performed by that person or team who has been assigned first otherwise much time can be wasted when another person would take charge from an earlier one. Only one person should be responsible for completing one activity.

13

CONCENTRATE ON ONE WORK AT A TIME

I start this chapter with a quote. A student of class 10th standard was very laborious in his study. He was also very scared about each and every subject of the study in spite of his interest in a few subjects. That's the reason that he keeps open books of all the subjects on his study table so that when any difficult point comes to his notice of any subject, he might be able to see that point in the respective book of the subject and overcome that difficulty. His parents, perhaps also consider his style of study in the right way so never interrupted. Now, what happened near to exams, confused at the large and passed with 20th rank in his class out of a total strength of forty students against his deserving position of 4th or 5th. This might be the reason that he couldn't create his mental focus on one subject.

According to behavioural psychologists when one does multitask at a time, this style would cost him

40 percent of total productivity. Handling at a time more than one work does not prove your activeness of doing all works. But more chances are there of multi errors and inhibit your creativity when you perform in multi-task. Single-tasking is the opposite of multitasking and it's better in virtually every way. Also working on one thing at a time lets us dive deeper and perform a better job at task. Although switching rapidly from one activity to another causes loss of a minute but over the course of a day, these minutes accumulate to a significant loss of time.

So far, I know from senior management, lesser chances are there when they stress the others to multitask at a time and report about that. This is so because they know what outcome might be there from such execution. So rarely they may instruct until there is dire need or urgency of the particular work. Such a style of working may be one's individual choice or habit when either he makes the attraction of others while doing a number of tasks at a time or he is totally confused which is also not good for completing the work. In both cases, the loss remains to be of the organization either in the way of a number of errors or loss of productivity that might be of any level to the wastage of time. So far, in my opinion, this may be a psychological problem of one's health & mind which needs medical treatment.

The administration should notice such happenings if it exists particularly when the matter is of payments or receipts. If one is in a leadership position, delegate some duties to any of the other responsible staff. Even if your work is not managerial, you can still explore the possibility of hiring a virtual assistant or a freelancer. If the undertaking doesn't require a personal touch, you can save time by hiring someone else to do it while you prioritize other duties. Or, you can always use the time to relax. Such a step might even make you feel happy. As a Harvard researcher reported to The New York Times, "People who spend money to buy themselves time, such as by outsourcing disliked tasks, reported greater overall life satisfaction." (source: google search)

Summary

Tight hold on particular work is only possible when you do all work one by one and this would also save time in a big respect. Even a student can't command the subject if he carries the study of all subjects together.

14

UNDERSTANDING OF WORK - MAY BE INTERNAL OR EXTERNAL & REGULAR UPDATION THEREIN

A perfect driver can reach you in time while an untrained one, may he run the car at faster speed than the perfect, need not be mentioned here about the possibilities that he can do. So, time can be saved in doing work only when one is perfect in knowledge, experience, or understand the line of action that should be adopted in the performance of respective work. When any work may be of productive or non-productive nature being performed with little or half-knowledge, results may be pre-seen as regards to wastage of time, expenses, and sometimes the whole next process also based on the previous one. In such cases, time is not only a waste of people involved in completing that work but also of others due to non-completion at the previous end. To increase the knowledge or understanding of work, one should also be familiar with the new techniques of performance or about those innovations also that are available in the market. Efforts from the organization are also preferable when they arrange meetings to provide knowledge to the working team with logics of every step of working. These efforts certainly help in understanding the internal procedures of doing work within the organization.

Knowledge of those works which have to be done outside the organization is also important to save time in performing those work. Without proper knowledge of how a work should be started, then compliance of all the required formalities, completion of entire documents of the file, the right person to whom follow up be taken, internal guidelines for completion of work by the staff of that concerned department/office, etc., one may wonder without any mean from here and there and wasting time and money due to lack of his/her knowledge. Proper understanding of getting done all the external work sometimes becomes so important when whole commercial activities can be started only when required NOC or approval etc. could be obtained in favour of the business entity from the respective departments or departments.

Summary

Employees need to understand the role of their work.

If one can't understand a work, better would be to assign the same work to someone other who is able to do that. In continuation of above said quote, if a person does not have a reasonable understanding as of others while learning how to drive a car, better it would be to let him do the work on the two-wheeler as he was doing earlier. Otherwise, there would be equally wastage of time not of him but also of driving school, the fee paid or other expenses, and the probability of an accident if he continues doing mistakes while driving the car.

15

TEA BREAK OR LUNCH BREAK AFTER FIX INTERVAL & FIX TIME

To the best of my knowledge, every business enterprise provides half to one hour's break for lunch to its employees and supposed that after four-hour work they would have some food and relaxation from the work so that he/she might get himself/herself ready for next working period at the respective workplace. It is so because no one either physically or mentally can work at 100% capacity at 100% of the time. This is a good activity being carried out by the perhaps almost all small and big enterprises where they may either take rest, gossips with colleagues, or do some personal work and be free from that work stress. Improvements in this regard may be added if management feels any need therein.

So far as tea break is concerned, from my point of view here are some improvements that are required not only in a few of the organizations but in a large number thereof. As per existing practice normally tea is served near to fix a time at the work station particularly if I talk of those staff who are working in the office. They take their tea along with working at the workplace and normally are not allowed to leave work which they are performing. If I talk of lower-level business entities, say shops, showrooms, or other small manufacturing concerns, particularly of a retail selling point, here the time of serving tea is not normally fixed and staff used to take tea when they are not occupied in dealing with customers. Now, in such a situation, if time can be fixed for serving tea as well as a five to ten minutes break, and be officially announced to all working hands, would be much preferable and might boost the work efficiency of the whole working team which would ultimately save time as well. During this break, time staff can relax a little from the monotonous work and re-equip themselves for the next hours' work. If we consider the existing system where no official announcement on tea break has been informed, can we be sure that staff is doing continuous work while taking tea simultaneously? Perhaps not! Even in the presence of seniors, junior staff leave the work to go and gossip with other colleagues or play on the mobile, etc. with the only difference that all this happens unofficially. Senior manager normally overlooks such things as he is also in favour of some rest as he is also a human being. Here I would like to mention that I do not mean that during such tea breaks staff should go somewhere out of their chair for this tea break. They should remain at their work station, take 5/10 minutes to relax in either way after taking tea and restart the work. This small rest would definitely improve their work performance not even after taking rest but also before going on tea break because it would remain in their mind that now it is tea break time, so to have more comfort, first complete the work in hand and start another work after the break with a fresh mind. One can argue that this is only possible only in the case of senior officers or managers of the organization. I also agree with it but still feel that there must be some improvement in performance although one is doing fix and routine work may be of a junior level. This might be possible with a psychological effect on the human mind.

Summary

In my childhood, I was used to listening from my parents that 'REST IS BEST NEAR THE TEST'.

Or even today when I am writing this book, my daughter again and again asks me to take a little rest to freshen your mind for new thoughts.

If I talk of myself while writing this book or the other, I myself do fast to complete the ongoing para or topic when I was to take a break either for tea, food, bathing, or others. In my view time definitely would be saved if the above said breaks are officially announced in the organization according to its circumstances.

16

PAYMENTS OF BENEFITS AT FIX TIME & AS AGREED

This concept indirectly improves the performance of employees or others associated with the business enterprise who are working for the organization. As I had said that this concept impact indirectly, by face impression one may not be in a position to judge any ambiguity from such persons who have not been paid their payments in time, but their working if carefully be observed, show negligence, procrastination of work or causing to some hindrances due to which work could not be done so far or in time.

Now, these people may be an employee of the concerned organization or a consultant in any manner who takes care of working of the business outrightly. Non-receipt of salary or other benefits in time creates chaos between them which directly reduces their performance in work. So instead of saving time by using various techniques implemented by the organization, excess time results in performing the same job as earlier. This may be due to the reason that employees couldn't be able to maintain their mental presence as of equal level as they can maintain, had the salary been paid in-time to them.

Similarly, a number of works of the organization had to be get done with the advice of outside consultants who are not on the payroll of the organization but perform equally important duties in running the smooth operations of the business entity. These professionals or other consulting firms also have an expectation that their payment would be received in time or a little bit late at a specified date but not likely that there would remain uncertainty in receiving thereof. If such situations occur it has been noticed that these professional firms start to linger on the work of that organization under the shelter of some excuses and time consumed is more as compared to earlier. Not only this, but sometimes big loss also occurs due to non-happening of some work in time from external sources.

Summary

Timely payment helps in maintaining the level of concentration at an equal level and to the specified.

17

ANALYSIS OF SELF WORKING

Self-analysis is also called self-examination, self-contemplation and self-concept, which consists of both our own evaluation as well as self-assessment of our performed tasks. But the true self-introspection is what others evaluate.

Time can be saved if every employee analyses his/her work daily and finds out his either mistakes or areas of possible improvement by the implementation of which a certain level of efficiency can be improved. I generally advise that if only one minute a day can be saved from the previous days' work, then after a month, half an hour would be saved when we accumulate only one minute of a day. Doing today's work in less time by one minute than the previous day working seems to be possible in the maximum kind of work definitely if not in all types of works.

Analyses of own work are considered to be best as no one else is involved in advising the earlier who is doing work in his duty. One need not mind this situation because there is no one else who has pointed out his mistakes to him in the respective work except himself. This exercise should be made at all levels of employees. If an entrepreneur considers it fit, he may also perform this exercise where he remains involved in the whole day may be in meetings, operational analyses, resolution of problems or in future planning etc. By his/her this action, he/she would definitely be able to think better on the performance of the same work to be executed in next meetings and also in a more efficient way than earlier. He may also think about other factors like his overreaction or loss of patience somewhere in those meetings.

This process may also be used by those employees of an organization who are engaged in performing duties out of the work premises. These people may be of sale, purchase or carrying liaison work outside the offices. A careful plan over the work by these people makes their jobs to be completed comfortably and without so much of running from one place to another. Rather they may reduce their out of office visits to the minimum by making their line of actions in a more and better way gradually and reduce the wastage of their time, energy and expenses also.

Summary

Self-observation of our own performance is a difficult task and people shirk to do this as they are not mentally ready to know about their mistakes. But if we consider the time-saving in self- analyses, this can save our good time and correspondingly other expenses also.

18

KEEP TO THE POINT

Time can be best managed or saved if staff or other people particularly of junior staff remains limited to his work and do not poke his/her nose in those matters which are not linked with him/her directly. This kind of attitude at workstation restricts him and others to be concise to their own work and not waste his energy or concentration in those areas which are not linked to him or his team. In the absence of this culture, working people may be involved in the matters of others and perform at a lesser level than the standard.

Some smart people involve themselves in the work of others, may be of the same department or of others and represent themselves as a good go-getter also about the work of others. This generally happens in non-production areas, say in the departments of administration, account, finance, PRO, sale or purchase, etc. and to some extent in the production department also. If we leave some of the cases of successful working by other people, there are more chances of thrashing about of specific work as neither the earlier one complete that work due to the involvement of other in the assumption that now new entrant would complete the balance work so he becomes disinterested in that job nor the new one many time complete the job who may take the excuse that I have given advice only and execution was supposed to be completed by the real assignee. If we leave the interpretations of both the person, loss of time and non-fulfillment of compliance occurs to the organization only.

To continue more in the same context, one further point in the favour of saving time goes to limited and necessary talk within the working team. This is also called the 'Be Brief' approach and has also been mentioned in the shape of a full chapter in my business advisory book. A talkative person or staff member does not only waste his own time and affects his performance badly but also of other teammates at that working platform. On the medical ground, high gossips are not so recommendable as loss of energy becomes the other reason to discourage as a human being has a limitation of this. Instructions should be passed on and the same be strictly followed by all. Only this approach if followed properly can save much of the working time and performance of the work can also be improved in any of the activities.

Summary

So far as business enterprise is concerned, everyone associated with the concern may be as employees or otherwise, should be particular and limited in his/her areas which have been assigned by the top management. Your competency in more than one area is definitely preferable but it should not disturb the existing system of allocation of jobs. You may bring to the notice of management about your extra capability of doing another job through the prevailing channel to convey the information and wait for till intimation or instructions comes to you as per system. Or a request can also be made to the management of your interest in having additional charge of that work in which you have proficiency also instead of directly intervening in others' work.

19

EASY AVAILABILITY OF TOP MANAGEMENT TO SENIOR TEAMS

Working teams need instructions when it has to start some new work with regards to the course of actions to be adopted for completing the work, utilization of resources, deadlines, external co-operation, and organized systems. Immediate guidance concerning line of actions should be provided whenever require them while carrying on work execution as per assigned duty. Each mission, whether it is regular or irregular, involves the efforts of the whole team depending upon their level of duties and responsibilities, and it may require interaction among the team starting from top-level to junior or say up to supervisor level. Need for such interaction increases if the work assignment happens to be of a new contract where customization requirements have an edge over the routine nature work. Now to comply with those specific requirements, foreman, supervisor, Engineer, Sr. Manager, AGM, DGM, GM or CEO have to interact with each other either in the organisation's hierarchy or by-passing some levels if there is an urgent need to resolve the obstacles. At this time, the availability of everyone pursuing the project becomes quite necessary and immediate to tackle the hindrances that might arise from time to time in completion of that work. Even if work is of routine nature, complications may still arise any time during the execution process.

Now the availability of senior managers around the clock becomes necessary to the junior staff. Here one thing can be noted that the above-mentioned whole context does not refer only to the production process of the organization. There may be another department, say accounts, finance, administration, human resources, public relations offices, or so on where the need for the opinion of seniors or their permission may arise all of a sudden and immediate action is required. In the absence of the same, actions couldn't be performed which were supposed to be, had the senior manager been available at the time of need for a necessary decision. Sometimes this non-availability becomes the reason for a big loss in monetary terms as well as wastage of time because when a task is stuck, the subsequent scheduled works also get stuck automatically.

We are committed to performing each work

efficiently and also know that junior staff might not be in a position to take the right decision as per his competency. Secondly, he is not generally authorized to decide at their own end, so seniors should provide time to his working team if not directly but in the level-wise of hierarchy definitely. Although the availability of seniors every time might not be possible because they also need a few uninterrupted moments when he turns off his phone and shuts the office door, when there is high probability because some work is going on where complications can arise anytime, then availability of the seniors becomes a must for necessary discussions. But every time he should not put his communication media, maybe laptop or mobile on airplane mode.

Summary

Keeping the target of best time management or say saving in time, it becomes necessary to do away with all the hindrances in working first. After this, the concept of efficiency can be thought over at the second stage. This can be possible when decision-makers remain available for taking the problem immediately. To digress a little from my topic, seniors are also supposed to be to keep their team productive and motivated towards achieving the goals. Accordingly, they stand by them every moment, make them understand, reward/punish, and manage.

20

MINIMUM NEGOTIATION

Negotiation or bargains takes too much time of the people engaged in this process, not only of the executing team but also of managers, senior managers or even entrepreneur also as this becomes the joining of two or more parts to discuss how to reach common interest and goals. If we once restrict our negotiation approach to the price factor only of buying material and leave other terms of contract silent or fix, even then too much time and energy of the business people lost in bargaining to mature that transaction. Although a number of products are there which are being traded at Commodity Exchange these days and online also but still in practical cases the only reference of rates is being taken and material is being purchased directly in B2B transactions by the organizations. This becomes also necessary because there are so many specifications other than the price factor in the purchase of raw material required by an organization in accordance with their finished products. If we talk of basic raw material i.e. iron or steel scrap, rates of the product depend upon the contents therein of moisture, dust, carbon, nickel or copper in percentage to the total quantity. Products with a high value of contents have more rates as compared to low-value content. This becomes the reason for the involvement of senior staff including the entrepreneur himself while buying the material from the market so that best rates can be settled. Now the process of negotiation starts. This takes good time generally and some time huge time is being devoted by the management in similar types of transactions that are not rare but in routine.

We need to be notified of these cases where time is being wasted in a bigger term. A systematic study, analyses and conclusion drawn therefrom might be able to save the time of all the team in so much of routine matters. I agree if fully this concept in any business enterprise might not be possible to be implemented due to speculative market or otherwise, but definitely, a minimum consensus may be established between buyer and seller with certain **FORMULAS** so that all the factors of cost of product need not be discussed every time of each transaction. If I continue the above quote of iron, nickel or copper etc. a consensus can be established on the amount of freight/shipment, GST, customs duty, other taxes, percentage of discounts or premium, percentage of each composition etc. might be fixed once for a longer period till major changes occur in any of the factor and daily rates of that item being quoted at a certain platform to be taken as a base rate for above calculations. In such a way, the buying would become a systematic procedure for all those who are engaged in this process. And if all teams are not available at any time for finalizing some contracts of either buy/sell of material, people sitting at distinct places can manage the transactions easily & in the interest of the enterprise. If such a formula can be established for the maximum type of transactions may be of sale & purchase, much time, as well as energy, be spent there, can be saved by the enterprise team. Many of the organizations are already in this process of buying & selling either partially or completely and devoting less time in such dealings in routine.

Please note that in all the above said transactions whether, of sale or purchase, whatever non-bargaining approach be implemented, this would not save the time of one part only; rather this approach would equally save the time & make work easy for the other counterpart also.

Summary

If we see with a long vision on the concept of no negotiation, we may find a number of other benefits associated therewith in the long run. This I had already elaborated in my book on business advisory and even had mentioned that if negotiation is possible to be eliminated, a business can run on automation mode.

This style of business would save the maximum time of the entrepreneur and its team from routine work and can invest the same in other significant areas of the business.

21

EARLY SETTLEMENT OF DISPUTES

While we carry on some business, either in goods or services, it is a general phenomenon of arising conflicts or disputes in day to day working. These issues may be small or big which sometimes go to respective courts for their settlement. Small issues do not disturb our businesses greatly and are generally settled mutually or by the mediation of some arbitrator commonly known to both parties or else.

A problem arises when a dispute enhances to an extent that it goes out of the boundaries of business premises or circles. Now expenses/losses start incurring directly and indirectly to the organization. Sometimes these disputes rise to a high level where such cases continue for a long time and even in the higher courts. This creates heavy losses to the business directly and loss of time and concentration of higher management/entrepreneur indirectly. Or say such petty or major cases eat up enormous sums of money, time, concentration and talent. Without adequate concentration and sufficient time, how can one grow in his/her business? It would not be wrong to say that even the existing business becomes difficult to maintain at its pace at which it was running before the start of such a dispute. Very careful and hard concentration is required at this time to keep continuing the smooth running of the business. In a number of cases, business goes down due to these prolonged pending cases either in one department or another. These disputes not only cause us to incur financial loss rather damage relationships as well as tarnishing reputations of the organization. A reasonable compromise to settle these disputes remains preferable even when there are chances of equally winning but after an indefinitely long time.

Many countries have considered the benefits of early dispute resolution and have also made efforts towards the recognition of decisions in various cases of civil section and compoundable offences of criminal cases if a compromise is being done out of court. However, their courts have the right to quash such orders particularly when these are against the social interest.

The American Bar Association Section of Dispute Resolution has appointed the Planned Early Dispute Resolution (PEDR) Task Force to promote settlement of disputes at the earliest and to take advantage of the services of neutral dispute resolution professionals in this regard.

Summary

Disputes become the reasons for heavy wastage of time as well as concentration of the entrepreneur from the routine activities and growth oriented strategies.A single dispute takes lots of time of a number of people, may be internal staff or the others. Settlement of disputes should not be kept pending.A businessman is not meant to avail benefits from some kind of disputes even if he might be sure about his win and have benefit of a good amount. Even after winning, you wouldn't have the same level of interest in business as that of before. I am constrained here in mentioning the names of some cases who have suffered greatly in their businesses due to these disputes.Whenever such a case seems to occur, do your level best to resolve it at the earliest even though you have bright chances to win if the amount is not so lucrative.This can be done by availing services of some arbitrators, conciliators, mediators, business associations or some near and dear ones. One more consideration that should also be taken in this regard is to ''must consult about the outcome of your case before going into the nitty-gritty of the court's long procedures.

22

TIME SPAN OF DOING A JOB

Time has its own value particularly when one is engaged in commercial business may be of goods or services. The more time one can spare without compromising on existing running business, the better it would be. Time can also be spared when work is either completed in time or before time but not late than expected. This concept is applicable more to staff or other associated persons of an organization instead of the labour class workforce.

Many times, it becomes the practice of executives to delay the work as much as possible. The reasons behind such kinds of activities may be one or another. I am hardly concerned with those reasons, rather we are to see that work should not be delayed due to the negligence of persons involved there. This may be either due to a lack of their knowledge to do that job or making a fool of the organization as well as the owner also by manipulating the work every time they are asked about the status of that job. It is obvious that the owner himself/herself remains busy with the number of other assignments of the business and due to limited human mental capacity, he/she can't recall every talk which he/she has been told in an earlier meeting by the same executive. Such clever guys may CONFUSE the owner by narrating new stories every time or making different excuses for non-completion of the work. Sometimes they present a small segment of a particular work in such a big term, say work of 2/3 hours, they quote in the number of days to complete. Owners due to their busy schedule or absence of their full concentration while taking the report from those executives do accept what he/she informs in a rapid way & they leave the owner's office in hurriedness.

There are a number of quotes on this topic out of which one or two may be described here in below. In one case a job of lien mark (for the requirement of a particular bank) on the property of the organization was to be registered from the revenue department which was of three/four visit jobs to the revenue department. In the first visit documents as per the knowledge of the executive were to be submitted to the dealing clerk with a request letter and simultaneously asking him if there is any shortage of papers or other information required for lien mark. Although this should already be in his knowledge as two/three times he had already got the same work done for some other purpose. If we consider that he is doing this job the very first time, there are more chances that some documents might have escaped from submission to the revenue department on the first visit (although such info. is also available on the internet). So, we consider that in the second visit, he completes all pending requirements. In some countries, government staff are not too punctual or sincere in their duties. So, I assume that the said dealing clerk does not meet him the first time when the executive of your company goes there for work. On the whole, let's assume that the executive had to visit an additional two times for the submission of those papers. Means in four visits he completes all the requirements of the revenue department. Now internal official work starts in the department. Let us assume the department informs the executive that it would take another ten days to complete the job, so come after ten days when it would be ready for dispatch with the dealing clerk. It means after four visits in the last 3-4 days (one visit takes a maximum of 2 hours), now nothing is there to be done till the next ten days are over. Again, after ten days I assume that the dispatch clerk didn't send the document on his own, but had to collect from him in two rounds (which is now of one hour or one and half hour, as just to ask whether that respective document is ready or not).

By considering that the required documents say request letter, bank letter, copy of registry, property deed, etc., which was submitted to the revenue department, either had been ready by other staff at the back end or the executive himself collected/ prepared all those documents, total time in preparing and visiting would not be more than four or five full days at the maximum. Many times, when one goes out of the office for some work, he performs one or two other tasks also, particularly when such an executive who is doing PR (public relation) work of the organization also.

After understanding all the step to step procedure of doing the above said job, now everyone can estimate the genuine time that should be taken in completion of such a job. I have seen that in some organizations, time for doing such a job takes ten times more than we have considered. This is only because the owner does not have time or could devote his/her concentration to understanding the respective work's methodology and accepting what his/her employee told him/her.

Summary

As you have seen that how a simple work lingers on by the smart people and is manipulated to the owner. In such situations, it remains better for the owner, to consult some other person who has the experience of this work so that you may ask your executive if he/ she is taking more time in completion of the same work. If an entrepreneur does not want to go in much detail due to either shortage of time or otherwise, understand some procedural steps in a broader way which a department generally takes to complete the relevant work and your executive would not be in a position to manipulate you to a large extent.

23

AVOID UNNECESSARY EMAILS IN CC OR WHATSAPP MESSAGES TO UNCONCERNED PEOPLE

Concerning Emails or WhatsApp, what I have noticed that emails are being sent to a number of other employees who are either little concerned about the contexts of that email or totally unconcerned but the sender is sending the mail in CC or BCC just for their knowledge or to save himself in that position if any issue arises on him for the negligence of any kind. In such situations, he takes the shelter of intimation to so many people that he had mailed in that context to so-so persons of the organization and management can ask any one of them. Sometimes a number of receivers reach to five or seven in numbers who are rarely concerned with that mail. Now the things that would happen is, everyone involved in the mail have to read the respective mail and either speak in hushed tones that what was there be need to send it to me by the sender or unnecessary enjoy on the contents of that mail-in taunting way with other colleagues and waste his time as well as of others sitting with him/her. If this case happens with more than one such receiver then imagine, how much time is being wasted without any reason.

Similar is the case of WhatsApp when a message is being forwarded in a group consisting of a number of people. WhatsApp groups are common almost everywhere to make the conveyance of any message convenient to the number of people by one sender to save his/her time and it is right also. But it is seen that a number of times a message which was supposed to be in the knowledge of one person or a few persons is also sent in a large group of the organization which breaks the concentration of all those who had been added in that group when a ring turns on. The result is that the time of all those non-concerned people of that organization gets unnecessarily wasted which can be easily avoided. Now if the other people are not so sincere in their attitude, they may interpret the matter in their own way to other colleagues and enjoy the matter without any concern.

Summary

One best way to overcome the above-said problems may be of emails, WhatsApp or other social media is, to create simultaneously one common email directly under the control of either of top management or of MD office where one copy of all official mails be sent by the sender along with those person/persons to whom he wants to be. This copy will be considered for record purpose instead of sending to other ¾ persons just for the sake of evidence. Similarly, all official WhatsApp messages can also be intimated by default to a common pool for the sake of record when one employee passes information to others on WhatsApp within the organization. Although I am not clear about the possibility of such an option under WhatsApp, it might have been implemented in the system. This kind of common pooling of information in any organizations would help to save in time for a number of persons who are least concerned.

24

MINIMUM POSSIBLE PERSONAL CALLS, WHATSAPP OR MEETINGS, IF POSSIBLE

As I had described earlier in chapter 11 and chapter 16 regarding the importance of concentrating on one work only and keeping to the point respectively so that output at a given point of time can be accomplished with higher accuracy and quality. The same logic seems to be correct when we talk of avoidance of personal calls, WhatsApp messages or meetings while working at one's own workplace. Personal calls of employees should be restricted to a minimum or can be made during lunch or tea breaks as mentioned in chapter 13 of this book. Unwanted WhatsApp or other messages from unauthorized third parties disturb one frequently and highly.

Why should these personal calls be avoided? Many times, I had to bear arguments from the employees section that it hardly makes a difference on work if a few personal calls are attended at the workplace or personal meetings happen with our near and dear ones periodically. Friends, my opinion is different to some extent. If I talk about myself, my whole concentration gets disturbed if I take a personal call even for a few seconds. If as per arguments, once these few seconds be ignored from wastage point, much time thereafter is wasted as my concentration remains diverted for the next hour or half an hour (depending upon the matter) although I try to avoid such diversion be heavy on me and my vision seems to be engaged in my own work doing before that call. But still, the output of that level does not come had the personal call not been there. We are all human beings and cannot be deprived off from our personal lives. So, diversion of concentration becomes obvious whenever some small or other bigger matters occur there. They bring down our output during the period of such diversion. Personal meetings with our known, also impact likely and linger on various works may be in production or in non-production departments, when such meetings are held in routine at any level of employees of the organization.

One more thing is here to be noted that such loss of time or concentration does not remain limited to only the concerned employee. If I talk of not so senior-level employees but of other colleagues or junior staff who take a deep interest in those personal talks, if one whispers to their teammates, much of their time gets wasted by these people. In such a way the list of time wasters becomes longer than the only one concerned who had such conversation either on phone or in one to one meeting. And if the matter is of lust or similar nature, this spreads so fast at the workplace like a fire in the forest.

Summary

In today's scenario, all of you would fully agree with me on this terminology when parents are under tension that their children devote maximum time on WhatsApp, Facebook, Twitter, Instagram, etc. by using smart-phones. On the other hand, entrepreneurs are also suffering the same problems concerning their employees. If I say that to some extent use of WhatsApp, emails or Google has become part of business as well as of professional life, even then this is not recommendable in the lower level working people who are less conscious about the value of their time and if find opportunity do not hesitate to use these things at the frequent level. They go into personal talks so long even when they are on duty.

Similarly, personal meetings at the workplace need to be avoided. In rare cases, these can be arranged at the reception area or mini-conference room. Attending personal friends even of senior officers should be neglected which might be followed by good hospitality. This conveys non-professional culture to the others and much time is wasted of the relevant employee himself and of others whose concentration also diverts in observing those meetings. Moreover, if one does this at his own work station, the other colleagues may also follow the same practice.

Discourage all such meetings and calls to the extent possible from the working culture of the organization except in emergency situations otherwise, these can be possible in break times.

25

BE SURE THAT ALL SYSTEMS ARE IN ORDER

Any business enterprise may be of goods or of services that can-do work in complete form only when the number of other activities is being performed in order there. These activities are necessary and work as a support system for the main activities. Without these supportive infrastructures, no business entity can work in perfection as well as in time. Following departments are normally responsible to carry the core activities of any organization. These may be the production department, electrical and other maintenance, packing area, storage, administration, accounts, finance, sale, purchase or others, etc. if I talk of the respective enterprise engaged in the manufacturing of goods. In service industries, these departments may be the executive department, business promotion, customer relations, technical team, administration, account, finance or HR, etc. All the mentioned activities in both these industries require proper back up of various ancillary services for their smooth running. These supportive services need to be set in a proper system that coordinates all the core working departments in priority wise so that their working couldn't be interrupted due to the non-availability of any supportive services.

With the help of these established systems, all the departments plan their schedule of tasks accordingly and to the convenience of the next process in the line. Even the account/finance department would perform when purchase bills from purchase, store, material inspection departments would be cleared before their accounting in the books of account. The smooth running of production would only be possible when there is sufficient raw material, regular power & water supply, adequate repair & maintenance services, lifting of finished material in time to make sure of vacant space for a new batch of production or so on. A number of so many examples may be mentioned here in this context. Even any administrative or accounts/finance department cannot perform in time if power back up is not there & power remains frequently off in that area. Similarly, with disturbed Internet connectivity, the IT department would regularly face problems and all other departments might shout on it when they are unable to run their systems & use the internet facility. May I take now that you all might be able to understand the terminology of the 'systems in order' so far.

What happens when any single connection of this whole chain gets disturbed due to any negligence or mistakes by any executive of the working team, the whole of the next process stands stuck and all plans mature out of schedule? The above disturbance does not only happen in manufacturing industries only. Rather the same type of disturbance, as well as wastage of time, is also very possible in case the system gets out of order in service-oriented industries also. On the other hand, today's market pushes entrepreneurs to be work-ready at all times and all places.

Summary

In the view of not to make this book too long to read, I have condensed the chapter of "System in Order" in one chapter by way of merging two topics i.e.

1. System should be in order for the availability of required materials for core working departments.
2. System should be in order for the availability of required non-material things say services etc. to all the departments.

The working of any organization should not be disturbed in the absence of the above two things. Otherwise, a good time can be wasted.

26

KEEP THINGS AT RIGHT PLACE

But an orderly home looks clean at a glance – whether it actually is or not.

A good time spoils in just finding the things, working papers or other tools while working in routine. This happens only due to the negligence done by the same team or other while carrying the work in the previous shift, previous day or in the past sometimes. Many times people work with a casual approach at a workplace or in offices and do not care about the importance of small things like keeping the things at the same place specified for those tools, files, records or other equipment which remains part of one's working. Some organizations do not care about such tiny matters and also do not listen if a member of the working team also points out such mistakes to their seniors. In the absence of a materialistic response from them, the complainant leaves the matter to future and do not inform again on such negligence and things remain to continue as these were going earlier and sometimes also be a part of such casual system when he feels that nothing is going to be changed in spite of his or their best efforts as senior management is not ready to understand that what level of time is being wasted from such small negligence which can easily to be improved.

This happens not only in manufacturing industries but there are equal chances of such occurrence in service-oriented industries as well as in trading units also. Here senior staff remains intense due to negligence on part of their juniors while handling various important files, office records, data of various matters and so on. Chaos is created when either of records couldn't be found out at the time of their requirements and whole staff gets busy leaving their own work in between to trace out the misplaced things due to urgent needs. Had the clerk or PA or other responsible staff kept these records at the right place after their last use, time of so many people as well as concentration, would not have got wasted in immaterial work. Moreover, you can also imagine the level of irritation or fretting being suffered by either seniors or sometimes the entrepreneur himself. Such things do not waste only so much of time as is visible rather waste in multiple of 2/3 times in in-visible point of view when senior officers do not be able to concentrate fully on their next work.

To deal with such problems some techniques named as KAIZEN & 5S can be implemented in the organization. Kaizen is a Japanese term meaning "Continuous Improvement" or "Change for the Better". Involvement of all employees & this business philosophy might help to improve the operation process. Kaizen contributes to productivity & in methodical ways. A 5S methodology is a systematic approach for the workplace of the business enterprise as per five steps of Sort, Set in Order, Shine, Standardize and Sustain. 5S provides a positive environment for all, as well as a sense of security. You know where things are, and you can trust they'll be in their proper place when you need them.

Summary

Placing things at the right place is a small habit among employees which can be easily maintained by a little effort. Companies who are so professionally managed, the occurrence of such incidents happens to be quite less as compared to other middle level or unorganised concerns. Time can be much saved if properly placed things are used regularly in routine working.

27

SMART OUTFIT

"Time saving with smart outfit". Someone may feel quite awkward with this suggestion. But the position exists there. Loose outfit deteriorates the efficiency in work which leads to low output in the end. Since ancient times, the dress code has changed by a great extent while working at business workstations. As and when an organization finds the necessity of proper dress up position for its workforce, do not delay in the implementation thereof. Thinking of top management is now being gradually on proper and comfortable dress for their employees working in the majority of the areas of the organization. As I have seen that all the business concerns where this concept has been activated, never reversed their decision at any stage later on. Even the equal regulations are being maintained for female employees also.

Can we expect an equal level of productivity from an employee who comes in a bathroom slipper with loose clothes as compared to those employees who are joining their duties in proper dress code, comfortable shoes, active as well as handling free fitting. Earlier mentioned concept was a practice of ancient time which gradually remained converted in the modern scene just to overcome the shortcomings therein. Proper fit monkey dress has become the preference of those employees who are engaged in more physical work may be on machines, engineering or infrastructure etc. Similarly, people working in the office premises are expected to come in smart outfits with shoes instead of the said chappals. Even a small business entrepreneur or an owner of a shop/general store prefers to come to his work station in a formal trouser/pant-shirt with shoes instead of loose-fitting lower with T-shirt that he wears at home although there is no one to object to him. People have realised the benefits in terms of more work with proper outfit instead of loose clothes that need to be taken care of/handled whole time and concentration diverts in non-working areas which ultimately reduce the efficiency and results in more time.

Certain areas like security personnel cannot be expected to do their duties in loose dress and without shoes may be in sky, earth or marine and this is universal truth which anyone can see. Some people are of the view that the clothes you wear, affect your mental as well as physical performance also. Research work happened till now had also accept the biological impact of clothes when one put a smart fitting dress than the other one.

Summary

We can't run faster and longer wearing bathroom slippers.

Inspired by my own experience, I elaborated this concept which is able to improve work efficiency as well as working for long hours. Workforce of any kind and sex can result in fast with their smart outfit.

28

STOP RECALLING OLD MISHAPENNINGS & FRETTING

Is there any social need, some statutory requirements or other kinds of benefits that can be complied or get matured if we recall all those things that happened in the past with us that may be in worse shape? We either blame our luck or to so many other factors depending upon case to case and narrating other people of all those losses that had been incurred due to either one reason or the other. Rehashing painful memories is not good for anyone. By doing this, one only loses his/her present time which may be encashed in terms of good results had the same might be used in the interest of the business by way of better planning, new innovations and watching the market trend of their industry. Every time thinking or talking about our past, particularly of our bad events, only leads to demotivation in business in the present time and moreover discourages us to start new ventures or make expansion in the existing level as risk remains associated whenever an entrepreneur initiates new business or diversify in other products. Due to this reason, their growth gets stuck at the existing level which is not are commendable situation for an enterprise.

Many of our adages also take a plea in non-remembering of old bitter things that these acts only generate negative energy at the workplace which is supposed to be non-desirable in any case may be of a small enterprise or big. On the contrary, positive energy is always preferable particularly at a business place and even at home also. I know this topic is going outside of my subject of Best Time Management, but spreading my know-how in the interest of our people forced me to write such things here and somewhere else also at other places in this book or another book. However, readers are entirely free to consider the matter as per their own.

Summary

Do not waste time of yours or others by quoting again and again those bad moments in one's life or in business which cause huge losses to the person and his business concerned. Such thoughts, in my point of view, do not stand in good terms in the business which is supposed to be of an energetic person. Instead of recalling these things, analyse your experience of those bad memories, review our own mistakes, methods of improvements therein and conclude with the best opinion for the future ahead. Definitely, much time could be saved with the contribution to add value to the business.

(29)

DO MORE WORK IN SINGLE ACTION

"To kill two birds with one stone" rather I am of the opinion if we as well as our associate people are so active, energetic, experienced and intelligent then try to kill three or four birds with one shot. Despatch a single action that takes effect on more than one. It means to try to throw a stone at that time when two or three birds are in the same line so that each one could be targeted. The same I advise to the business organizations while carrying out various routine or other works. A good time can be saved if the whole work ahead is properly planned with the best line of actions. A number of employees least care about these plans and rush to do a particular job whenever it comes to them. They do not even care about the need for that work to the organization or the time limit within which this work can be accomplished. If these things are determined prior to the start of the respective work which has a good time when these would be required, the other ancillary or same nature work can also be planned simultaneously and be performed together comfortably. By doing this kind of plan all those works to be completed ahead in the coming time, can be started or run together in one and the same process.

Doing more work in a single round or single line of actions not only saves time but other expenses and concentration also. When three or four out of office works are together planned to be done in a single round of visit, saves every time of cost of conveyance to the organization instead of every time running out of office when a single work arises which can easily be postponed in next days. If I talk of big organizations, whenever someone has to go for errands, normally process remains of filling of a proper slip in printed format, getting approval of senior for official leave, sign-on out register at the gate and handing over the official leave slip after noting the status of KM Meter of a vehicle with the security staff. The same process with lesser 1/2 steps had to be performed when coming back to the office. Now one can imagine how much time can be saved if two, three or four works can be possible in one visit or say in two visits. Time of the whole of the machinery engaged in completion of the job, in an above-said process which has been implemented by the organization, would be saved easily along with other paper costs or conveyance expenses. This type of planning is expected from the senior level officer who has assigned the duty to the junior.

The same process can be adopted when outstation or out of country tours are planned by the organization and normally senior management or entrepreneurs are also involved in these works. In these visits, expenses involved in travelling increase by manifold for the organization. A little care can save a good amount of time as well as expenses also.

I have mentioned two examples above when some works to be performed out of the office premises where travelling time, as well as expenses, can be well saved. It does not mean that this approach can't be used by people working inside the organization or workplace. Particularly when civil work is going on, plant and machinery is under construction, during manufacturing processes where one process takes the same time and expenses up to a level of production, meeting with vendors, payment day etc. All these jobs can be planned to be completed in one through instead of again and again to save the maximum time of people.

Summary

One just has to handle single action across multiple. To bring the said concept in implementation, there is a need for a proper plan with the thin mind of seniors or top management. Their self-understanding towards this can benefit the organization in a bigger term if we accumulate all the benefits together.

30

DELEGATE YOUR WORK IF OTHERS HAVE CAPACITY TO ACCOMPLISH THE SAME

Every employee of an organization's family does his work as per his assigned duty and responsibility. These works are generally being performed by a team of employees in each department. The size of the team may be small or big, depending upon the size of work. In the electric maintenance department, may 3/4 people be sufficient? On the other hand, in the production department, a hundred or more employees might also be reasonable to carry out production. A similar case happens in other departments, such as Purchase, Sale, Handling of stores, Accounts, Finance, HR, etc. where a team of some employees works together in the joint operation of that department. Senior employees or employees are supposed to be aware of the whole working procedures of their team being carried out by them. But all the down line teams can't be supposed to be in reverse order. Still, some of the supervisors or assistant managers who act entirely upon the instructions of their seniors, come to know the maximum working style of their seniors. However, this is not known in a day or so rather in a long time of working with seniors. Much talented junior staff is expert in some kind of works that are being performed by the seniors with their help and support.

Now my subject starts i.e. ofTime Management, where I believe that those work or works which juniors have capacity to perform, might be transferred to them with responsibilities. Seniors need to ask themselves what they are doing, does it really need to be done by him, others can't do the same? If a junior is able to handle that work comfortably without any risk of damages, seniors would find his time free to that extent. As we know that every challenge first comes on the table of seniors and he remains responsible to make up those challenges. So, after finding himself free to some extent, he can devote much of his precocious time to handle new challenges or tackle the other problems. In this way, high cost-oriented time would be saved in one term along with monetary savings. Job interest, as well as the morale of those employees, would increase in the other term. Not limited to this, sometimes it has been observed that senior staff feels monotonous with his routine work when they become proficient by continuous practice and require some change. In all situations, the organization remains in profit.

Summary

The time of seniors, as well as the high cost of doing a job, should be saved when some work, maybe in small parts, is delegated to the junior team, which has the capacity to do the same in a safer mode.

31

AVOIDANCE OF EXCEPTIONAL INCIDENCES, LEGAL CASES & OTHERS

A general quote is that "ALMIGHTY SAVE US FROM DECEASE & COURT".

Up to now, I have stressed on the occurrence of all the routine matters of the business where time can be best managed if some care is taken by all the teams of the organization and particularly by the top management who are responsible in implementing the policies and procedures for the working system. These works can be best judged at the pre-occurrence thereof.

But happening of exceptional nature things, perhaps can't be predetermined so rightly and in some cases absolutely not. These situations may be of natural calamities, change in government rules and regulations, arising out of disputes either of people concerned with business or with others, and many times litigations get started either of civil nature or of criminal nature. Whenever either of the above or any other not mentioned here, any such incident takes place to the organization, too much time goes in vain without any reason. Cloud bursting, floods, earthquakes, fire, or many others are examples of natural calamities and disasters. Similarly, government actions in the form of search and seizure by the Income Tax Department, GST, Custom Duty or Enforcement Directorate may also create trouble for the organization. Disputes with associated or non-associated people lead to police actions or long pursuing court's proceedings etc., de-concentrate the management from their target and time and money wastage also be there.

If I count the wastage of time only, perhaps not be possible either for me or for any other. Every one deals with any of the above-said matters according to his own understanding and intelligence. Time and money involvement depends upon the line of actions which we adopt as per the common consent of our expertise. Now, if this action plan is of ultimate level, obviously time would less be wasted in these matters which occurred all of sudden and involvement of expenses be accordingly. On the contrary, the reverse position would be there, we are to do our efforts to the best of our capabilities to resolve the issue without much involvement of legal actions against us. Long litigations are entirely not recommendable for both the parties of vs.

To avoid much disturbance to our business from natural reasons, we may take necessary and available precautionary steps beforehand to meet any contingencies in the future. To cover the risk of natural calamities, adequate insurance coverage is best considered to make up our losses to the maximum extent. However, some pre-arrangements to reduce the effects of such disasters might be provided in the workplace.

Although the above said incidents can't be predetermined exactly and other efforts either prior to the incident or later can save us from high losses of time and money to the lowest possible level. But one thing that might be done by all of us along with the above-mentioned safeguards is "PRAY TO ALMIGHTY" so that we do not indulge in any unlawful activities and remain safe from all those calamities or sufferings that occurred otherwise. When God stands by us, nothing bad can happen to our business or family. Along with praying to supreme power, also do beneficial work for the nation and society and be a good citizen of our country.

Summary

No summary, except to Pray.

MESSAGE TO THE READERS

It is obvious and self-understandable terminology that any limited thing should be used wisely in the context of more and long-term benefits. The same is the case of Time Utilization wherein increase is next to impossible as we require. To optimally utilize this limited thing, one should avoid time wasters or say, thieves. Identify these culprits and keep them away.

Some people are very successful in their business as well as in their lives. But it does not mean that they are all good time managers also. Managing your time well makes you successful.

By: Ben Franklin, 1748 - 'Time is Money'

Auto Mode: Time and overhead expenses be best saved when automating workflow processes are implemented in the workplace. This proves to be the key to achieving these two goals. Putting the Business on auto mode provides a number of other benefits to the entrepreneur and enterprise itself. This process does away with all the hurdles in the smooth running of any business, provides satisfaction and motivates the top management to add more value to the growth of the organization by utilizing their surplus time.

GLIMPSE

- When the word CLARITY comes, the word CONFUSION gets over by default.
- Fixing clear duties, as well as rights, require a high-level of concentration based upon past experience, nature of work handled and practical situations that might arise from time to time in one's business in addition to other factors.
- Clear work refers to an exhaustive term which denotes the overall work plan of a business entity while clarity about duties refers to the work that each member of the team is supposed to have in his/her mind to perform as per the instructions of the management.
- Would it not be right that in respective meetings we 'Lock at least those points which had been discussed there, commented by all the presentee and a common decision had been drawn out therefrom?
- Doing things at the last moment always remain expensive that costs the company.

- Some flexibility must be there in all the procedures laid by the organization because in routine one may find chances to do the work in lesser time if he breaks those procedures with the permission of seniors.
- But still if somehow any training like 'Art of Living' or other can be arranged fortnightly or monthly, the benefit would go to the organization when the employee would work efficiently.
- According to behavioural psychologists when one does multitask at a time, this style would cost him 40 percent of total productivity.
- Although switching rapidly from one activity to another, loss a minute but over the course of a day, these minutes accumulates to a significant loss of time.
- A perfect driver can reach you in time while an untrained one, may he run the car at faster speed than the perfect, need not be mentioned here about the possibilities that he can do.
- Definitely, a minimum consensus may be established between buyer and seller with certain FORMULAS so that all the factors of cost of product need not be discussed every time of each transaction.
- Discourage all such meetings and calls to the extent possible from the working culture of the organization except in emergency situations otherwise, these can be possible in break times.

- Supportive services need to be set in a proper system that coordinates all the core working departments in priority wise so that their working couldn't be interrupted due to the non-availability of any supportive services.
- The time of seniors, as well as the high cost of doing a job, should be saved when some work, maybe in small parts, is delegated to the junior team, which has the capacity to do the same in a safer mode.
- "To kill two birds with one stone" rather I am of the opinion if we as well as our associate people are so active, energetic, experienced and intelligent then try to kill three or four birds with one shot.

END

Saving in time or best Time Management is a very detailed subject and can be elaborated in as much detail as anyone may require. I do not think that there is any segment related to business where time management can't be implemented. If someone agrees with me, even in the thinking process time can be either saved or additionally incurred if the thought process is not up to mark. We all have noticed that there are some topics that ever remain unresolved although they involve regular thinking of the number of people on the same matter. This process continues for a long time just to find out the seek solution to that problem. Many times, it has been noticed that the solution of the problem comes with a little effort by a new one who accidentally gets involved in the captioned matter. Why does this happen when a number of experienced people remain unable to find solutions to that problem but a new person resolves the same very instantly? Is this being a medical terminology that strikes in our brain all of a sudden or is talk of the Process of Thinking?

If it is a process of thinking, then definitely it denotes that quote where if one couldn't find a solution with his wisdom and experience, starts to rethink as a layman over the subject. That's why I am always in favour that Time Management is not supposed to work harder and longer.

DISCLAIMER

The views expressed in this book are those of the author(s) and do not necessarily represent the views of anyone else subject to some reference from news and other types of communication either from newspapers or from other media respectively. The contents of this book have not been written intentionally to target any one or more of any of the organization, class, creed, any workforce, staff or personal sentiments of anyone from anywhere, except to make these contents in an understandable form in general terms. If still anyone feels hurt coincidently by linking his individual opinion or other sentiments with any part of the book, I apologize to the same to that person by heart.

ABOUT THE AUTHOR

[B.COM HONS., FCA, DISA(ICA)]

CA R. Kumar, also known as Rajeev Kumar Garg, who is a commerce graduate & chartered accountant by profession along with another diploma in system audit, after 27 years' experience in different capacities either in full-time job or as a self-employed professional consultant and as an entrepreneur, put his hand in writing this book by conceiving whole of his judgements, perceptions, self-business experience and other things which he has felt, realised & analysed during the tenure of his career with final results of a particular problem/issue.

He has also been awarded "jewels of india" award in 2019 by international business council &indian solidarity council and has also received distinction in business managementaccounting during his academic career. "Siliconindia" a leadingbusiness enterprise & technology, us-india magazine, shortlisted 'mak growadvisors' for "best consultations and advisory companies to work for2020".

The entire book has been written purely on his thoughts which he extracted by using his extrasensory brainpower from the individual organization's management systems along with solutions thereto. This all has been done while simultaneously working for his livelihood due to limited resources. Before writing on business advisory, he also engaged himself in a business (for self-experience) which had been established with a little money & now developed in a good way with the handsome business conglomerate. Simultaneously putting his business on auto mode to the maximum possible extent & doing his job also, he continues his study in best management of time so that operational cost can be reduced as well as more work can be completed within a set time which would help the business to grow further in all key corners.

It is his opinion that if one has an extra sense or brainpower to understand other people's worries, he can give them golden advice.

He is also an advisor founder of a business advisory firm named as mak grow advisors (makgrow) specializes in advising the business entities on their problems and disputes resolution. To know more about the kind of services, one may visit at www.makgrowadvisors.com or call 9815610806.

www.ingramcontent.com/pod-product-compliance
Lightning Source LLC
LaVergne TN
LVHW020638100826
845148LV00012B/2223

* 9 7 8 9 3 5 5 4 3 2 4 7 6 *